Crystal

Mysticism

Crystal Mysticism

Lindsey Elizabeth Day

First published in the United Kingdom in 2023 by

The Cloister House Press

ISBN 978-1-913460-61-7

The photograph on P.83 is by Arthur Ogleznev care of
www.pixels.com

*P*ronouncement

**This book is dedicated to
EORRESH YAVOY**

**I lift up my heart and I lift up my eyes
to the One whose wisdom is far greater
than all the wisdom possessed by all
who are wise**

$\mathcal{P}$rogramme

$\mathcal{P}$ortmanteau

P*oem*

≡<>≡

Learn to dream when thou doest wake,
Learn to wake when thou dost sleep...
Plough thou the Rock until it bear,

Know, for how else couldst thou believe
that all things,
by immortal power,
near or far,
hiddenly linked
to each other are..[1]

≡<>≡

[1] From: The Mistress of Vision by Francis Thompson

$\mathcal{P}$rologue

The Jewel of Consciousness
is in the Heart Lotus

OM MANI PADME HUM MANTRA

When we were in Eden, the garden of God, before we descended to the physical plane and took on human form, we were perfect. We were full of wisdom and every precious stone was our covering; *Sardius (Carnelian)*, *Topaz* and *Diamond*; *Beryl, Onyx* and *Jasper*; *Sapphire, Turquoise* and *Emerald* with *Gold*. We walked back and forth in the midst of *Fiery Stones* and we were perfect in our ways from the day we were created[1].

Once we began life on the physical plane, a ladder was set up on Earth. It reached into the heavens and Angels of God could be seen going up and down the ladder[2]. A mysterious document was found recently that allows all humankind to gain access to a special rung of the ladder again. This permission was withdrawn a very long time ago due to the misuse of the power of sound and crystal power as well as forces that were far more powerful than could be understood in human terms.

[1] Reference Ezekiel 28:12-15
[2] Reference Genesis 28:12

The document re-emerged on 22.2.22. In numerology, twenty two is the master builder number and it is associated with the world and turning goals into reality. Two represents balance and harmony, peaceful participation in world affairs and nurturing Earth. When all the numbers of the date, 22.2.22, are added together and a single number is obtained, the number arrived at is one. It signifies a new beginning.

It was foretold, a long time ago, that a Great Event was going to happen to our Civilisation, but "fire, brimstones, doubt and ladles of the soup of cast off woes" would all come before a Great Light shines down on the inhabitants of Earth. On 24.2.22 Russia started a war with Ukraine.

The system of thought that belongs to the lower planes of consciousness will be abandoned when Humanity's Great Shift occurs. A higher level of heart consciousness will come into our beings; our human bodies will become more crystalline and our light bodies will be able to be seen by everyone who is living on the physical plane as well as those of other beings; for the next phase of development of human consciousness will be governed by the unseen becoming visible.

The crystalline nature of the light body and some of its attributes are set out in the first paragraph of this text by using the names of certain crystals. Some crystals have been described as the 'angels' of the Crystal World because of their qualities and some gemstones are said to be the 'archangels' of the Crystal World. This is because they are deemed to be the earthly representation of Archangels' Rays. For example, Archangel Uriel's name means, 'The Light of God,' and *Rubies* are associated with Uriel because his ray is the *Ruby Ray*. *Emeralds* are connected to Archangel Raphael as his ray is the *Emerald Ray*. His name means, 'God Who Heals.' *Sapphires* are linked to Archangel Michael because his ray is the *Sapphire Ray*. His name means, 'He Who is Like God.' *Diamonds* are associated with Archangel Gabriel as her ray is the *Diamond Ray*. Her name means, 'God's Strength.'

At present we are only able to relate to the World of Light via symbols, signs, metaphors etc. We have to have images that are like something or someone in the material world. For centuries we have likened The Divine to a loving Father. Understanding, however, needs to be gained that in the Almighty One there are numerous Light Patterns and that means our languages are totally inadequate at portraying EORRESH YAVOY (Source/Absolute Love) or the Holy Spirit, Who has been described as a dove, a flame, a tongue of fire, the breeze, flowing water, and so on.

The words, EORRESH YAVOY, are from The Holy Language of The Light. It is also called, 'The Cherishing Language,' as it is the expression of the outpouring of the warmth of God's Love. Information about the language can be found in the Portmanteau Section of this book under Parlance. Once the Great Shift occurs, all of us will be re-attuned to the language. Wave after wave of higher frequency vibrations, from the language, will then be conveyed to us and knowledge will be passed over to us about things that have been a mystery to us for ages.

Gemstones and crystals truly are a wonderful gift from the Universe. They can improve our understanding of the World of Light now and they can also help us to gain access to our inheritance. My *Citrine Cluster* looks like a pile of gold nuggets. It reminds me that where my heart is, that is where I will find my treasure. Whereas, in my opinion, the *Spirit Quartz Cluster* that I have represents the warmth and love of the gentle Breeze of Spirit, the Protector and Comforter.

In a poem called, 'The Jewel,' the Persian Poet and Mystic, Hafiz, revealed that if there were no seekers after *'Rubies,'* the radiant Sun would pierce the dark 'mines' that He chose to pierce and then the stones in them would be set ablaze by the Light of the Sun. Leading up to the Great Shift, the number of people who are regaining understanding of the mystical properties of crystals and gemstones is increasing.

Some gems and crystals can only be properly attuned to whilst in the meditative state as the energy of these stones vibrates on a higher spiritual frequency. One of them is a *Quartz Crystal* called, *Azeztulite*. The volume and content of the knowledge that flowed to me when a connection was made with the white variety of this crystal resulted in this book being written.

My connection with crystals began during past lives in Atlantis and Ancient Egypt. Atlanteans and Ancient Egyptians were well known for being able to utilize the powers of crystals and gemstones. They did this by communicating with the spirit in the Light Bearer and in my book, ATLANTIS: AS BELOW SO ABOVE, A

SPIRITUAL ODYSSEY, I included information about *Quartz Crystals*, Thoth's *Emerald* and the way that *Diamonds* were activated. All the knowledge that is in that book, as well as in CRYSTAL MYSTICISM, was revealed to me whilst I was meditating.

Before you set off on the mystical expedition, I am going to share with you details about the *Crystal Skulls* and Figurines that have played a part in the extraordinary information that I have received as well. They have helped me and they may help you, too, to gain greater understanding of how everything created has a spirit, whether it is manmade or generated by natural means. Crystals are also called rocks, minerals and stones and some people even refer to crystals as 'stone beings.' It can be a fascinating experience to make a connection with the 'personality' of a *Crystal Skull.*

The *Clear Quartz Skull* that I have has a masculine type of presence. The skull made it very clear to me where it wanted to be put on my meditation table as soon as it arrived in my home. When I asked the skull what name it wanted me to call it, I was surprised that it wanted to be known as 'Fred,' but it does suit the skull's personality.

In contrast, the *Amethyst Elongated Alien Skull* that I own has a feminine presence. As soon as this skull came to me it transmitted that it would speak to me as long as I responded to it gently and in a kind, loving, respectful way. I promised that I would do so and I was then made aware that I was to call the stone being, 'Asinthi,' and that the name means, 'One who has gained an extraordinary level of insight about The Light.' It is a joy to see the way

15

some *Crystal Skulls* light up when you communicate with them in the Language of Love.

A question that has been asked many times is, 'Why do *Crystal Skulls* look like human skulls?' It seems to me that my *Clear Quartz Skull* represents the ultimate expression of the human being. The Great Shift will mean that we will also be in contact with numerous other realms, just as some skulls are, and because of the level of cosmic consciousness that we will possess then, we will be able to instantly access the vast amount of knowledge about The Light that will be available to us.

With regards to my *Amethyst Alien Skull*, my understanding is that there is at least one other planet that hosts a humanoid type form. I was made aware that the elongated skull signifies that the beings who reside there are more advanced than those of us who live on Earth. In their skulls the two worlds, which can be equated to the two hemispheres in our brains, have merged into one world. They do not have a subconscious level of consciousness so there is awareness of everything all the time; hence the shape of the alien skull. This amount of information would be too much for the human brain to process yet.

Extraterrestrial Beings have been visiting Earth, in various forms, since our universe was manifested. As each new stage of our development has been about to take place, Heavenly Beings/Extraterrestrials have provided us with knowledge beforehand and made us aware of any signs we should look out for. An example of the knowledge that I have received telepathically, whilst I have been holding Asinthi, is as follows. 'She' told me that Al-Haram As-Sharif/Har HaBayit, the Dome of the Rock in Jerusalem, will need to be evacuated. When I asked why that will be necessary, I learned that a seismic event will occur there. It will cause the Dome to be split in two, and the mysteries of the Rock will be exposed. The level of peace that will arise will enable progress to be made. In other words, peace will demonstrate the advanced state that the Human Race will have reached.

If crystal skulls are programmed and used correctly, that is to say not only for our own personal benefit but also for the benefit of all humankind, they can be wonderful spiritual mentors. During this time of change, they can provide a wealth of knowledge to help us through the process of the reconfiguration of our beings so that they are attuned to the higher frequency that Earth will be vibrating on as a result of its Great Shift.

One of the life changing components of Humanity's Great Shift will be a 'renewed' sense of our higher selves, in other words, who we really are. I have a figurine that is a depiction of the Ascended Master, Quan Yin. She is revered as the Goddess of Compassion, Mercy and Absolute Love in Asian Culture. The statuette is made from *Labradorite* and across the back of the figurine is a yellow/gold zigzag, which I associate with the lightning strike/bolt. It represents the Holy Spirit quickening, in human beings, the higher emotions. I regard Quan Yin as the role model for the ultimate expression of the human being.

Apart from communication taking place with Ascended Masters and Crystal Light Bearers during meditation, other types of messengers, including Angels and Archangels, can make contact. Archangel Gabriel's twin flame is called Hope. The Angel of Hope figurine that I have helps to remind me that despite the increasingly dangerous dramas that are taking place in the material world, there is always Hope. Hope can steal away any doubt that a better world will emerge when the Great Shift occurs.

You may be wondering when this Great Event will happen. It will be when the Great Light appears and we hear the mega OM/AUM.

OM is considered to be the sound that brought our world into existence and it will bring the second 'Adam and Eve' into being. The inclination that is in some of us to start wars will be removed and the healing of the nations will take place. We will be provided with all that we need to sustain the level of perfection that will result as the Great Shift, from our current level of evolvement to the peak performance of our human selves, comes into being. The powers that will be restored to us will enable the true greatness of our Race to be realized.

On the next page is a photograph of another statuette that is in my home. From my point of view, the figurine highlights the crux of the Great Event.

I took this photograph of my statuette of Jesus in 2019. A flame is visible in the area of the Heart Chakra, the Throat Chakra is highlighted and amazingly a cross can be seen in the region of the Third Eye Chakra of the figurine.

The photograph below was taken in 2022 in the same way. The change that has taken place can easily be seen. The symbol on the forehead is now extremely bright. It looks like a Pi Symbol instead of a cross.

Pi is a magical number as it is limitless. It signifies the infinite within the finite and it is a sign that indicates that the New Dawn of The Light of the World will be occurring soon. Humanity will then embark upon a monumental journey into divine consciousness and an enhanced relationship with the Source of All Wisdom will ensue.

I am now going to help you to get ready for your journey into the World of Light. During the expedition, you will be able to hold a special crystal, which is kept in one of the vaults where your treasures are stored, and make a wish; search for a priceless *Pearl*, and find out about stones that will be re-discovered as a result of Earth's Great Shift.

PLATFORM NO. 1

*P*reparation

Salutations to the Great Purifier,
Who purifies and protects
the sincere seeker

OM VAJRA SATTWA HUNG MANTRA

Before a journey to another country is started in the physical world, preparations need to be made so that it goes as smoothly as possible. Travel documents and travel currency will be required for the journey and Tour Guides may need to be arranged to accompany you on your expedition. Your travel plan will certainly include details of the transport that you will be using. A vehicle may be essential to make a journey overland in your own country. You may have to board a boat and go across an ocean before getting into an airplane and flying to your destination. It will also be necessary for arrangements to be made regarding transport to take you back home. You will, more than likely, have to purchase some travel items such as a pair of new sunglasses, a bottle of suntan lotion, and even a book that contains guidelines about the place that you are going to.

The details that follow are about the preparations that are necessary before your spiritual journey can begin.

Travel Document

The travel document that applies to the expedition that you are going on is called, 'The Document of The Rose.' It is the mysterious document mentioned in the Prologue and its timely retrieval coincides with the rapidly approaching Great Shift. Many more rungs of the ladder will be accessible to us after the Great Event.

Travel Plan

The transport/vehicle that is needed to take you into the World of Light is meditation. Its gears are Light - Flow - Wisdom and even higher gears are able to be engaged when this mode of transport is used on a daily basis.

The first part of the journey involves getting on to the Wisdom Path. It is called the Wisdom Path because when a deeper level of meditation is attained, higher wisdom starts flowing to you from the Infinite Mind.

The path begins 'in your own country.' That is to say, it starts in the energy centre in your physical body that is called the Base/Root Chakra, and then goes 'overland' to your Crown Chakra. It carries on beyond your Crown Chakra and goes up through the Transpersonal Chakras to the Stellar Gateway Chakra.

Transcending the body is a liberating experience and it

rapidly increases the speed at which spiritual development occurs. Twelve chakras are involved and they are as follows:-

1.   Base/Root Chakra.
2.   Sacral Chakra.
3.   Solar Plexus Chakra.
4.   Heart Chakra.
5.   Throat Chakra.
6.   Third Eye Chakra.
7.   Crown Chakra.
8.   Soul Star Transpersonal Chakra.
9.   Spirit Star Transpersonal Chakra.
10. Stellar Gateway Chakra.

Although the Soul Star and Spirit Star Chakras are usually referred to as one chakra, the functions of the two chakras are different. The Soul Star Chakra relates to a more profound connection with the Great Soul of Light Supreme and the higher emotions and as a result, you feel 'at home' swimming in the Ocean of The Light. In contrast, the Spirit Star Chakra revolves around, amongst other things, the activation of an advanced level of connection with the Holy Spirit, and the impetus to ascend to the highest dimension that is possible. When the Soul Star and Spirit Star Chakras are opened up so, too, is the eleventh chakra, which is Earth's Soul Chakra, and the twelfth chakra – Earth's Spirit Chakra. This is so knowledge that has been obtained in the higher realms can be downloaded for the benefit of all of us on Earth. First of all, though, the Kundalini needs to be awakened.

There are various techniques for awakening the Kundalini/divine energy in the Base/Root Chakra. Kundalini is a derivation of the Sanskrit word 'kundal,' which means coiled. The divine energy is said to be coiled up like a snake until it is roused. Its movement up the central light column has also been likened to that of a snake; its movement through the Ocean of Light, which is accessed via the Soul Star Chakra, has been likened to that of a fish, and after the activation of the Spirit Star Chakra, it is described as soaring like an eagle to the Stellar Gateway Chakra.

My first experience of the awakening of the Kundalini occurred as a result of chanting the Sanskrit seed sound of the Third Eye Chakra, 'OM/AUM,' very many times. Although it occurred over twenty years ago, the experience is as vivid as if it took place yesterday. The divine energy travelled straight up my central light column at great speed and because my Third Eye Chakra had opened, I was able to see the energy exit my Crown Chakra as a spectacular fountain of light. I have experienced a heightened level of awareness of the World of Light ever since.

As gemstones and crystals are the travel currency for this expedition, a crystal rosary is used to activate the Kundalini so access to the Wisdom Path can be gained. You can, however, make your own rosary by attaching crystal pendants to a necklace, made of chains, with necklace clasps. The clasps can be purchased online from Amazon. Stones are chosen according to the twelve chakras mentioned in the Travel Plan Section. There are lists, in many books about crystals, of stones that are associated with particular chakras, but you may wish to choose stones according to what their attributes and colours mean to you. (Information about how to use the crystal rosary will be provided when the Tour Guide for the journey appears.)

Tour Guides, Spiritual Teachers and Those Who Watch Over Us

Not everybody is able to see those who watch over us. The photograph on the next page has brought much comfort not only to my family, but also to other people who have seen the picture, for it provides proof that we are watched over, helped, and continue to be cherished by our relatives even when they no longer reside on the physical plane. I took the photograph with an ordinary 35mm camera. It is of my daughter, son-in-law, and grandson. On the left side of the picture there are two relatives. Their features can be seen even though they are in the World of Spirit. My grandmother is on the left side of the door. She passed over thirteen years before I took the photograph. The man next to her is my son-in-law's grandfather. He departed from this world three years before I took the picture. I did not meet him whilst he was incarnate, but my son-in-law and his father recognized him instantly. White light can be seen coming from them. It reaches my grandson. About a year after I took the photograph, my grandson had a serious febrile convulsion. I am very relieved to say that both my grandchildren, who are twins, safely reached adulthood. My grandmother gave birth to twins and neither of them survived.

On the first occasion that Higher Beings of Light appear whilst you are in the meditative state, you may get a glimpse of their physical features if they are Ascended Masters, or they may supply you with a relevant piece of information so that you know who they are. When they visit you again, you may not see an image of them, but you will know who they are with absolute certainty. It was not until I discovered the teachings of Paramahansa Yogananda, though, that I stopped feeling so bewildered and amazed that esteemed Spiritual Teachers and Spirit Guides wanted to communicate with me whilst I was meditating. In one of Paramahansaji's books I found out that it is customary, whilst in the meditative state, to encounter, and be able to communicate with, Great Teachers. Often they are associated with the religion or mystical tradition that is being followed in the present incarnation, or it may be because of a connection with them in our past lives.

I was, nevertheless, completely unprepared for the meeting that I had with a Being who appeared to me a few days before a Reiki Master attuned me to the First Degree of the Reiki method of healing. At that time, I wanted to be a healer very much and I was eager to know more about the sacred Reiki symbols that are visualized as the healer acts as a channel for the energy from the Infinite Mind. During my research, I came across an illustration of a meditational aid called, 'The Antahkarana,' and felt compelled to draw the diagram that is below.

THE ANTAHKARANA

As soon as I had finished the sketch, I closed my eyes. There was nothing in the book to indicate that a visitation by the Being whom I saw was likely, but I knew instantly who he was because I could see him very clearly. He was wearing winged sandals and on either side of his hat there was a small wing as well. Mercury asked me what I wanted, but I was so flabbergasted at seeing him I was unable to respond. He seemed to be irritated that I had summoned him for no reason and disappeared.

Through the centuries various cultures have called this Being by different names; to the Egyptians he was Thoth, the Greeks referred to him as Hermes, and it was the Romans who knew him as Mercury. When an *Emerald* Tablet, which contained written instructions on how to change base metal into *Gold*, was allegedly discovered by Alexander the Great near Hebron, one of the oldest cities in the world, the information was attributed to Hermes Trimegistos or Hermes the Thrice Great. In the Coptic Gnostic text, which became known as, 'Pistis Sophia,' it was recorded that Jesus told his disciples Hermes' eternal name. It is, 'Tarpetanuph.' In spite of each of these cultures having their own name for Mercury, they all regarded him as a messenger and scribe to the gods because he brought knowledge to them about the alphabet, writing, The Mysteries, and many other things as well. The Greeks and Romans, by way of illustration, depicted him holding the caduceus, and it is still used as a symbol of medicine and healing.

Some years after the visitation, I found out that Mercury/Thoth was considered to be the founding father of a trust that was set up a very long time ago to make sure that the knowledge that was divulged by him was not lost during the carriage of time. Many souls, and many more of every kind, have been carriers of this knowledge. At a pre-ordained time a connection is made to the appropriate wavelength of the Infinite Mind, and the knowledge starts to be released so that it can be shared with our earthly companions.

The Tour Guide for your journey may surprise you. His name is, 'Melchizedek' (Mel-key-zeh-dek). You may recall that in the Holy Bible he was called, 'The Priest of God Most High' and that he was the King of Salem, that is to say, the King of Peace. Teachings of the 'Order of Melchizedek' have been passed down to initiates through the centuries as well.

Melchizedek is also called the 'Great Paralemptor.' In this role, he is a Receiver and Purifier. He receives the Light that is brought into the Treasury of Light and purifies it so that the level of consciousness that there is of The Divine can be expanded. In order to meet him, a meditative state has to be entered into.

Transport

There are worlds within our world and meditation can transport you to them. As a consequence, meditation can bring magic into your life every day that has a lasting effect.

To assist the process of entering into the World of Light, I use the items listed on the next page. If you are able to purchase them to help you, it is important to be aware that they are never to be employed for any other purpose.

Transport Requisites

Tingshas, Tuning Fork for Crystals, 2 Singing Bowls*
A Bowl of Water
Rose Absolute Essential Oil
White Tealight or Candle
A *Rose Quartz* Crystal

* One bowl should have a slightly higher vibration

Tingshas/Crystal Tuning Fork/Singing Bowls

The Heart Chakra is the intersection between the human self and the Higher Self. The tingshas (Tibetan cymbals) are sounded over the centre of your chest with the intention of opening the Heart Lotus/Heart Chakra at the level that it is opened in the Higher Self. Information about the tuning fork can be found in the Crystal Section. The two singing bowls will be used at the end of the meditation.

Bowl of Water

Ideally the water that you put in the bowl should be spring water, but filtered or filtered water that has been boiled is acceptable. After the water has been blessed, a drop is put on the area where the Heart Chakra is located. It symbolizes the cleansing and purification of this energy centre. This is necessary because the meditation has a very special purpose. It transports you round the four chambers of the Sacred Heart. They are the Treasury of Light; the Parliament of Light; the Inner Sanctum of The Wise, and the Inner, Inner Sanctum of the Sacred Heart.

Rose Absolute Essential Oil

Rose Absolute Essential Oil has the highest vibration of all the essential oils. It needs to be used for this journey because it assists in the opening of the Heart Chakra at a deeper level so that the Holy Spirit can make contact with you.

Before anointing your Heart Chakra with the rose oil, you should always dilute the oil with base oil. For those who do not have a sensitive skin, five drops of rose oil needs to be diluted in 10ml of almond, grapeseed or jojoba base oil.

White Tealight or Candle

Candles/Tealights should be put in a suitable fireproof container and placed on a stable surface that is not near curtains etc. Always make sure that the candle/tealight is extinguished, using an appropriate gadget for the task, before leaving a room even for a second.

White is a symbol of peace, spiritual purity and rebirth via a gentle transition to a higher state, and a candle or tealight is a representation of The Light. Light Bearers can appear in a variety of forms and crystals are recognised as being one of these forms.

Crystal

Rose Quartz is associated with the Heart Chakra and it is held throughout the meditation as a reminder to view all that is seen with the 'eye' of the heart. Crystals are usually held with the left hand as that hand takes in energy, whereas the right hand tends to give out energy. This applies whether people are left or right handed, but if you feel more comfortable holding the crystal with your right hand that is fine as that is what is right for you for this meditation.

To activate the *Rose Quartz*, hold the crystal against your Heart Chakra first of all and give thanks to the Universe for this lovely gift; put a little drop of rose oil on a cotton hankie or a tissue and gently wipe the oil over all of the crystal to cleanse it; gently tap* the crystal with a 4096 cycles per second (cps) tuning fork to awaken the crystal's vibration, and then specify your intention for its use. You may wish to say a prayer such as this one with your inner voice:-

May all the good energies of this
crystal be activated for my benefit,
may it assist me with my journey,
and may enlightenment
come to the world.

This fork is tuned to the ninth octave of the overtone series and it can open the doorway to the Angelic Realms. On this journey, Archangel Gabriel and Archangel Michael, along with their Twin Flames, will emerge from their realms and give you guidance.

* Only 'hard' stones like quartz can be tapped with the tuning fork. For all other crystals, tap the fork above them with the wooden beater that is provided with the fork.

Transport Guidelines

In order that you will not be disturbed whilst you are meditating, you need to turn off your mobile phone, put pets in another room, and shut the door of the room that you are in. Next, set out the items listed in the Transport Section on a table that is positioned in front of you.

◇

If possible, sit down on a dining room chair. It will help you to keep your back straight so divine energy can easily rise up your central light channel from your Base/Root Chakra. Make sure that you keep both of your feet on the floor for the whole of the meditation so that you are grounded and can easily return to the physical plane when it is finished.

◇

Light the candle/tealight and say, with your inner voice, an affirmation of protection such as this one:-

I am protected and blessed by the
Loving Light of The Almighty
at all times.

◇

Sound the tingshas over the area of your heart chakra and then cup your hands round the bowl of water and say, with your inner voice, a purification prayer such as:-

Purify my Heart Chakra, I pray you,
Great Soul of Light Supreme,
so I may truly understand
what is revealed to me at all times.

Put your middle finger, which is your fire finger, into the bowl and put a drop of water on the area of your Heart Chakra.

◇

Next, put a drop of the diluted rose essential oil on the area of your Heart Chakra with your fire finger and say a prayer such as this one:-

Sanctify my Heart Chakra, I pray you, Holy Spirit,
so I may receive the whole light
and the whole power
of your Holy Gifts.

◇

Now that the preparations have been completed, as soon as you pick up the activated *Rose Quartz* you are able to see a deep pink light emerge from your Heart Chakra. This is because the 'eye' of your heart has opened.

◇

A flash of turquoise light is emitted next. It comes from your Throat Chakra indicating that the channel, which will enable communication with the Tour Guide and those in the higher realms, has been opened.

◇

A blaze of intense electric blue light then erupts from your Third Eye Chakra and you see a Being standing by your side. He is surrounded by gold light; framed by white light, and encompassed by force fields in which many spirals are visible. The power of his presence fills you with awe and it is not until he says, "Dear One, the journey is about to begin," that you realise that this Being is your Tour Guide.

PLATFORM NO. 2

$\boldsymbol{P}_{ath}$

**Salutations, Great Spiritual Teacher,
kindly steer us on to the path that
leads to the perfected being**

OM NAMA SHIVAYA MANTRA

To help you to get on to the Path and make the special connection with the Crystal World and the World of Light that is needed for the journey that you are about to embark upon, Melchizedek gives you a beautiful crystal rosary. He explains that it denotes that 12 chakras will be fully opened again in all of us when Earth's vibration is raised to the level that it vibrated on during the Atlantean Civilization; and that human bodies will become more crystalline again due to Humanity's Great Shift.

The rosary consists of a red *Ruby* as it symbolizes a passionate desire for an enhanced relationship with The Divine; a red/orange *Carnelian* as it sums up the feeling of joy that is experienced when travelling up the path to The Divine; an orange/yellow *Citrine* as it represents the wealth of knowledge that starts being opened up about

The Divine once the divine energy has travelled up the path; an *Emerald* with *Gold* as it associated with knowledge about the depth of the love and compassion that The Divine has for us; a green/blue *Turquoise* as it conveys a deeper level of loving communication with The Divine; a dark blue *Sapphire* as it epitomizes the primary function of the third eye chakra, which is the ability to see, at a deeper level, the beauty of the perfected being; a deep blue/purple *Amethyst* for it highlights the level of peace that needs to be obtained so the body can be transcended and direct experience of The Divine obtained; white *Selenite* as it magnifies our spiritual gifts; white *Phenacite* because it illuminates very old vaults that are now being opened so that we can gain access to treasures that have been stored in them until the Great Shift; white *Azeztulite* as it exemplifies the heightened level of awareness that is obtained after passing through the Stellar Gateway; black *Tourmaline* as its grounding properties are essential after visiting the World of Light, and black *Magnetite* because its magnetic properties assist in opening up, on Earth, profound realisation of far reaching possibilities; for when Hope is resident in us, it enables them to blossom into full grown actuality.

Melchizedek makes you aware that you need to gently stroke each crystal or gemstone in turn, starting with the *Ruby*, whilst repeating a mantra. The mantra is, 'Peace, deep peace' for the first three stones; it changes to 'Deep peace, deeper peace' for the next three stones, and the words 'Deep, deep peace' are chanted when the *Amethyst* is stroked. The *Selenite* crystal is held at the same time as the *Tourmaline* crystal and the mantra changes to, 'Very,

very deep peace.' The *Phenacite* crystal and the *Magnetite* crystal are also held at the same time and the words, 'Very, very deep peace' are chanted. Finally, the *Azeztulite* crystal is stroked whilst expressing the mantra, 'Peace, perfect peace, the peace that passes all earthly understanding.'

You realize that you have reached the Stellar Gateway when you hear your Tour Guide say, "Dear One of Soul Sight, you have arrived at last." Archangel Gabriel is by his side and she tells you that your Travel Document is in order and access has been granted to the *Diamond* Rung of the Ladder of Ascending Heart Consciousness. This is because there is a higher level of harmony in your Heart Chakra with the power of the illuminating Light of the Great Soul and the ascension Light of the Holy Spirit.

The Archangel opens the Gateway with her *Diamond* Ray and Melchizedek takes you into the highest dimension, which you are able to enter at present, of the Sacred Heart.

$\mathcal{P}$ilgrimage

**O Self-effulgent Light, Who has given birth
to all the spheres of consciousness; Who is
worthy of worship, and appears through
the orbit of the Sun, illumine our intellect**

GAYATRI MANTRA

The first chamber of the Sacred Heart is the Treasury of
Light. Your Tour Guide leads you to the area of the
Treasury where the vaults that contain your treasures are
kept. He removes a *rock* from the first vault and tells you
that this crystal was stored in the vault until you were
ready to channel its powers again, for it is very powerful.
Melchizedek informs you that it is called a '*Fiery Stone*'
and as he holds the rock up to the Light, you are able to
see that there is a flame within the stone. Your Tour Guide
gives you the crystal and asks you what it is that you wish
for.

You tell him that your wish is that Quan Yin accompanies
you to the Parliament of Light Chamber. You need to

deliver an important message to the Speaker and her loving support would mean a great deal to you.

Melchizedek opens another one of your vaults; takes out a garment, and asks you to put it on. It is a voluminous cloak of white light. When you put the hood on your head, the large *Diamond* on the hood is positioned over your Third Eye Chakra and rays from the *Diamond* surround your head.

Your Tour Guide then removes a *Diamond* ring from a third vault. As he returns the ring to you, he reminds you to put it on the third finger of your right hand as it represents the Sacred Marriage of the human self to the Higher Self and its many facetted relationship with The Divine.

When you put this ring on your finger, the rays coming from the *Diamond* are so powerful you watch entranced as they dance around your being. Now that you are suitably attired to go to the Parliament of Light Chamber, Melchizedek summons up Quan Yin.

The Parliament of Light Chamber

The light that is being emitted from Quan Yin as she looks at you is very soothing. Her tenderness came into being from having experienced much suffering in the lifetime that she experienced before becoming an Ascended Master. Tenderness cannot exist where there is bitterness. Tenderness comes from an understanding heart and it is radiating from every facet of her being.

Quan Yin gently enfolds you in her arms and says, "Your message will be most suitable, Dear Soul. Once there is a greater level of awareness of the plight that is being experienced by humankind, your message will be viewed with compassion. Understanding will arise of how to provide more help to those who are undergoing many trials and tribulations before the Great Shift. They are due to aspects of the human self being exposed that are not of The Light."

As you go into the Chamber, you realize that it is a hallowed place for it glows with a powerful gold light and you keep your head bowed until you are called to deliver the message. When you rise from where you are sitting, Quan Yin says, "All will be well, there is nothing to fear."

You look round the Chamber now and notice that Archangel Gabriel is in there. Your voice is strong and full of hope as you convey the message to the Beings in the Chamber.

"Dear Ones of Light, I am honoured to have been admitted to this Chamber in the company of Quan Yin as it is the quality of compassion that I am going to speak about.

"It is hard not to be filled with compassion at the plight of human beings in the 21st Century. All that has gone before should have been a wakeup call to us. Instead wars, poverty, racism, sexism and all manner of things, which should have been overcome by now, are still continuing. What awaits us is the catastrophe that these things engender. The misuse of the powers that we have been given has continued in spite of the knowledge we have about what happened to previous civilisations who did the same thing. The compassion of those of us who are prepared for the Great Shift gathers pace for those who are still not ready for such a Great Event.

"Peace (you express this word with great emphasis), peace in the hearts of all human beings? Is this possible with the threat of nuclear war hanging over us? It seems unlikely so we humbly ask that more is done to help us.

"Thank you for giving this matter your consideration. May we have your answer as soon as possible so that all of us, who joined together to make this request, know if it was the right thing to do."

You bow to the Assembly and sit down. Quan Yin gives you a big hug as the Speaker stands up. You are informed that a conference will take place straight away to establish the help that Extraterrestrial Beings will be able to give humankind now that they have asked for assistance.

Powerful energy starts circulating round the Chamber in the form of a tongue of flame as the Beings discuss the matter. After awhile, it alights upon the head of the Speaker who stands up again and says:-

"Raise your eyes, Dear Soul, and you will see two projections."

A series of images appear on the wall of the Chamber that cause you to gasp in horror at what you are seeing. A rapidly melting glacier is featured. You see forests wantonly being destroyed; people having to leave their homes because of natural and manmade disasters; fires raging uncontrollably; creatures who inhabit the oceans of Earth struggling to survive because of the pollution and, in addition, there is a strange wind blowing through the land masses that reminds you of the nuclear wind that occurs after a nuclear bomb has exploded.

The Speaker comments on this by saying that it is, indeed, a very grim projection of what is going to happen if action is not taken as soon as possible. It is also an extremely heavy burden for Earth to carry. You are advised that the Beings in this Chamber are aware of the effect that the fluctuations in energy are having on Earth Beings. Some people are confused, some regard it as ominous, some debate how it can be stabilized as they believe they are capable of handling everything that occurs in the material world. This matter defies logic, though, and unless they are spiritually advanced, they will not realize its true significance and that there is nothing that they can do about what is taking place. The preparations that are being made for the New Dawn of The Light of the World are reaching a critical stage. Adjustments are being made to the human configuration so that the ultimate expression of the Human Race can come into being.

A different set of images are then presented to you. The treasures that Earth possesses are being used for the good of all as a higher evolved way of life has been brought into being. Earth is thriving and as it revolves, gold rays are sent out for the benefit of others in the Universe.

The Speaker asks you which projection you prefer.

You are made aware that crafts will appear that will not be able to be destroyed by human weaponry. The time of their arrival will be known to those who are attuned to a channel of communication that will have been opened up so contact can be maintained with the World of Light. The vehicles will land where they will be needed most and their occupants will make it clear that they come in peace. They will help humankind to draw back from the brink just in time and assist their transition to a higher level of evolvement when the Great Light shines down on them. This response leaves you in no doubt that it was the right thing to do to ask for help.

You learn that on the Great Day, a long white cloud will part in the centre. The intensity of the Great Light will cause the ground to tremble and jolt. Its power will be felt as an electrical shock and the motion of all beings will be frozen. They will be unable to move so that they fully understand the magnificent power, the magnificent glory of The Almighty One.

A sound like a distant drum beat will be heard followed by a buzzing sound as the power of the Force increases. When the noise stops there will be complete silence. The silence will be even more frightening to some as they will know that something unprecedented is about to happen and that they will not be able to run away from it and hide.

The lightning strike of the Holy Spirit, which will be experienced by all, will be accompanied by a sound like the rumbling of thunder and the roaring of waves. The mega OM/AUM will pierce their hearts and as these words resonate and keep resonating in their hearts,

"You come from The Light;
remember now how your
being is made of light,"

they will awaken from the dream of human existence.

You are now invited to go to the Inner Sanctum of The Wise. This is so that you can learn about the 'seed,' which was implanted in humankind a very long time ago. It will be activated when the Great Light shines down on all those on Earth.

The Inner Sanctum of The Wise

Quan Yin takes you to the Inner Sanctum and the first thing that you notice is a huge multi-rayed star on the ceiling of the Sanctum. It feels as though you are being lovingly caressed by the rays that are coming from the star.

The Wise are three co-joined beings. They have a vast field of consciousness and are surrounded by pure white light. They have been waiting for you to visit them and they make you feel very welcome.

On a table, in the centre of the Sanctum, they have set up a model to help you understand what is going to occur. A ray from the star is being directed on to a vertical rectangular container that is filled with liquid.

The Wise tell you that it is crystalline liquid and suspended within it is a brain particle. They explain that what you are seeing is a representation of the Great Light activating the brain particle or 'seed' that was embedded in humans so that the Great Shift could take place.

You are then made aware that once the particle is 'switched on,' instead of divine energy rising from our Base/Root Chakras it will be projected from our Crown Chakras. This signifies that the focus of human beings will be on cosmic consciousness instead of human consciousness; the ego; the physical body, and the material world. The Wise impart to you that trillions of light particles will form into a figure of eight as a sign that the 'shadow self' in humans has been completely removed by The Divine. With the resetting of the flow of divine energy caused by the 'shadow's' release, they will be able to dedicate their lives to living in peace. The Wise expand on this by saying:-

Peace will be with the doubters; for their doubts will be cast out when the Great Light appears.

Peace will be with those who loved to cause disharmony before the Great Day. The unravelling of the gross nature is so a higher evolved way of life can be brought into being. They will realize that they had been destroying the harmony of their own souls, and they will make haste to live in harmony with The Light.

Peace will be with those who had been haters of womankind; for when they see the Great Light they will realize that the Divine Spark is in all that is manifested.

Peace will be with those who had not bothered to learn about their true nature before the Great Event; for on the Great Day they will be able to see the radiance of the light of the Higher Self.

Peace will be with those who had lost their faith; for what is real will finally be understood by them to be what they thought to be unreal.

Peace will be with those who had become disillusioned with the religions of the World; for a treasured wealth of knowledge about The Light will be obtained by all, and it will remain in Humanity's consciousness forevermore.

Peace will be with those who had clung to outdated beliefs; for the crumbling assortment of bygone philosophies will be replaced with newly valued wisdom that they will be able to assimilate with ease.

Peace will be with those who had been beset with negative thoughts. When the Great Light shines down negative thoughts will no longer arise; for consciousness will be attuned to the Higher Causal Planes where all thought comes from Divine Love, and the feeling of joy cannot be denied.

Peace will be with those who had been confused by the mysteries that have clothed the collective consciousness of humankind for so long, as all that was known about The Light before 'The Fall' will be retrieved and the Seat of Learning will be advanced.

Peace will be with those who had been dismayed at humankind's rate of spiritual progress since the First Coming; for when the Great Event of the Second Coming occurs, a glorious level of awakening will take place.

Peace will be with those who had been concerned about the nature of world affairs after the Great Shift, for values will change in line with the level of attunement that will be obtained to the higher vibration.

Peace will be with those for whom the loss of 'free will' had seemed inconceivable as they will realize that by letting go of their 'free will,' the radiant Presence of SHI and the gifts of the Holy Spirit that have been manifested in them are ample compensation.

Peace will be with those who had prayed for peace on Earth; for as the higher harmonies start resonating in human hearts and the asunder of the existing condition of earthly beings occurs, their energy pattern will be re-arranged to accommodate a higher vibration and the numerous obstacles to peace, which could not be resolved before the Great Day, will be no more.

Peace, deep peace will dwell in human souls as they awaken to the New Dawn of The Light of the World, and this will enable great things to be achieved during the next phase of the evolution of human consciousness. Knowledge will be gained that will benefit the whole of the Universe, and greater understanding of the environment will lead to a gentler, kinder management of Earth.

After you have thanked The Wise for giving you more information about the Great Shift, Quan Yin takes you to a different area of the Treasury of Light as it is time for you to start searching for the *Pearl*.

The Rose Window

Melchizedek is standing in front of a beautiful rose window. In the centre of the rose there is a magnificent *Diamond* and sparkling light is pouring thorough the jewel on to the stone that Melchizedek is holding up to the window. Your Tour Guide tells you that the stone is called *Moldavite* and that it has an extraterrestrial origin. It is known as the 'Stone of the Great Shift' because of the clearing that often happens when the stone comes in to your possession. This is so that an extraterrestrial level of consciousness of The Light can be opened up in you. He places a vial of sacred oil in your hand and advises you that you will be made aware when you need to apply a drop of this oil to your Heart Chakra. Melchizedek now holds the stone against your Third Eye. A vision of yourself standing on top of a cliff emerges, and you see that Archangel Michael and his twin flame, Faith, are beside you.

Michael explains that if you have been weighed down with many aspects of life on the physical plane that needed to be experienced but were difficult to contend with, they have to be cleared. This is to make way for something greater to come into being. He assures you that you will not be harmed in any way and once the clearing has taken place, the divine process will begin. You will be provided with all the help that you need to find the

Pearl, the jewel of consciousness will be grasped, and a renewed sense of being will be obtained. The Archangel shines his dark blue sapphire ray on the waterfall of light that is cascading down the cliff and you take the leap of faith. You land in a huge pool of sunlit light and bathe in its radiance for awhile. Subsequently, though, you are dragged down into an underwater passageway. It is an eerie place, but when you reach the end of the icy cold corridor, all your preconceptions, all your doubts and fears, anything that was stopping you moving forward and gaining fuller appreciation of The Light are within you no longer.

A great fountain of light erupts and you are deposited in the gnarled hands of an ancient being. The being has thin arms that are similar to branches and a long fringe covers the face of the being. The fringe reminds you of a weeping willow tree. Due to the expansion of your consciousness, as you look at the green light that is being emitted from the being, it occurs to you that this being is an Extraterrestrial being, and then it dawns on you that the being that you are seeing is the *Moldavite's* being.

The being touches your Heart Chakra to check that you are both on the same wavelength and then the spirit of the *Moldavite* starts communicating with you. Your Mentor makes you aware that a passageway is going to be opened up to you. It leads to the Inner, Inner Sanctum of the Sacred Heart. Next, you are informed that when you reach the end of the corridor you need to put a drop of sacred oil on your Heart Chakra from the vial that Melchizedek gave you. The 'eye' of your heart will open and, as a result, you will clearly see what you have been searching for. The

51

being conveys to you that there are many levels on which the Patterns of The Light of The Divine can be understood; but if your heart is open to accepting the way things are in the World of Light and the Holy Spirit makes contact with you, it is a sign that you have been blessed with Divine Grace.

Unlike the other passageway, as you travel along this passageway a lovely feeling of warmth penetrates your Heart Chakra and you feel at peace. At the end of the corridor there is a veil covering the Sanctum, but once you have applied the sacred oil to your Heart Chakra, the veil falls away and the new dawn of your divinity is defined; for something sublime is revealed to you.

In the Sanctum there is the most exquisite red rose that you have ever seen. To be so close to something of such perfection is a divine experience. Wonder fills your willingly opened receptive heart as you gaze at the rose; for its beauty is beyond compare; the power of its heavenly fragrance elicits a feeling of ecstasy, and as you touch the petals of the rose and feel their softness, your heart is pierced by a feeling of profound love and compassion for all beings. The outpouring of the expression of the Absolute Love of Source then starts flowing into your heart.

"I Am because I Am Love.
How great is this Love?
Love is All.

"My boundless Love
surrounds you at all times.
Its power protects your existence.

"I caress your mind and soul as
I tenderly hold and watch over you,
for you are precious in My Sight.

"I Am your Light, and Sole Redeemer.
I Am your Inspirational One.
I Am your Divine Right.

"I Am the birds that you see or
the Beings that you behold.
All are extensions of Me.
There is only One.

"I Am is all that you see.
I Am That I Am.
I Am SHI.

"I rise in the peak of your soul's
containment of Light.
I sparkle in the Light of your eyes.
I am within your soul and,
Beloved One, you are within Me."

PLATFORM NO. 4

*P*anorama

Salutations to the One,
for the power of the sound of the Voice of the One
brought Creation into being and the One is the
Bestower of all kinds of knowledge.

OM EIM SARASWATIYEI SWAHA MANTRA

The words, '*I Am because I Am Love*,' and '*I Am SHI*,' are still resonating in your Heart Chakra when you become aware again of being in the Treasury of Light. Melchizedek reveals that this renewed sense of being is because you are filled with the Light of SHI and as a consequence, the jewel of consciousness has been discovered. The jewel is Absolute Love for all and its facets are great compassion; loving-kindness and mercy.

He goes on to say that once this enthralling relationship with the Source of All Wisdom is opened up again it brings ever-new bliss; for the beauty of The Rose draws you deeper and deeper into the Sacred Heart and direct experience of The Divine is obtained at a more profound level.

Furthermore, your Tour Guide tells you that due to you being as One with SHI, the priceless *Pearl* that has been searched for by many people, in all sorts of places over the centuries, will now be found by you.

You feel that you are, indeed, blessed by Divine Grace because the Breeze of the Holy Spirit then wraps round you and the Name of SHI, which is

I-I-I mmmmmmm roo-oo-oo-oo-shhh inggg k-tahhh zzzer shoo-oo-oo-oo-shhh

is lovingly revealed to you.

In addition, as The Name is being conveyed to you, the gold Sacred Heart flame emerges and you can see that The Name of SHI,

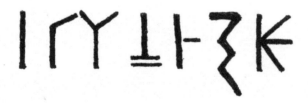

is hidden in a special place; for it is 'etched' on the Sacred Heart, in the Cherishing Language.

Melchizedek informs you that this priceless *Pearl* of wisdom sits at the centre of the *Diamond* Rung of Ascending Heart Consciousness; for once The Name of SHI is known, the level of spiritual wealth that can be amassed elicits amazement and true humility.

Seeing that you are sitting on the Throne of Higher Wisdom; you are in harmony with the ways of the World of Light, and you know about the depth of God's Love for all of Creation, Melchizedek imparts some more information to you about the Great Shift.

He starts by saying that the essence of the Great Shift is the expansion of the Love that is in human hearts. The pandemic opened the hearts of many people; the war in Ukraine opened even more hearts, and the crowds who gathered to honour the one whose dedication to duty was respected around the world demonstrated that the number of humans whose hearts had opened had grown exponentially. The use of the powers that had been given wisely and always from the heart set a fine example for the next phase of the preparation for the Great Shift and the realization of a more divine way of existence. What will follow will be the absorption of the next field of exemplary particles.

It was prophesized a long time ago that an apocalypse would take place. The crises that will be happening will be necessary for the survival of life on Earth. First of all, a massive volcanic eruption will concentrate human minds on the fact that Earth is angry at being badly treated. It will be understood that Earth is ejecting the toxic substances that have been put in to it with great disregard for its well being.

Shortly afterwards, a meteor that will look like a cannonball will enter Earth's atmosphere. It will bring the next field of exemplary particles that will transform the abiding force for a higher level of existence. The meteor will crash into an ocean and land, which disappeared a long time ago, will re-emerge. As human consciousness continues to expand, Earth will be inhabited by an advanced civilization; for all of humankind will experience, first hand, the Peace of the Merciful One which is beyond compare.

After you have had time to digest this information, Melchizedek provides you with some special mementos regarding your admittance to the Inner, Inner Sanctum of the Sacred Heart.

To sanctify your renewed sense of being, he places the *Moldavite* stone in your hand as a farewell gift and also gives you a medal. It consists of a *Pearl* in the centre of a *Diamond* that is in the centre of a rose. The *Pearl* shines with a lustrous glow. It is a reflection of the high frequency vibration of The Name of SHI. The *Diamond* sparkles with all the utterly lovely colours of The Light and your Tour Guide makes you aware that a wealth of knowledge about the *Diamond*'s facets is available to you from this time on. He explains that the rose signifies that direct experience of The Divine has occurred and that the medal indicates that the Diamond Level of Ascended Heart Consciousness has been fully opened up in you. Now that these gifts have been awarded to you, Melchizedek takes you back to your vaults.

PLATFORM NO. 5

$\mathcal{P}$arting

I Am Divine Love

AHAM PREMA MANTRA

When you reach the vaults, your Tour Guide asks you to place the accoutrements in them that you needed for this expedition. This is so that you can use them again when your next journey into the World of Light is booked. He explains that there will always be higher rungs of the Ladder of Ascended Heart Consciousness to climb so that an even more profound level of resonance with The Divine is obtained.

Once you have placed the vial of sacred oil in the fourth vault, Melchizedek puts a *Gold* breastplate on you. In the centre of it there is a large square red *Ruby*. He makes you aware that a channel has been opened up to Archangel Uriel so that information can be relayed to you once you are back in the material world.

With much love and affection, you thank Melchizedek for being such a wonderful Tour Guide. He accompanies you through the Gateway and then he watches over you as you return to your temporary home on the physical plane.

After you have put your earthly mantle back on again, tap the singing bowl that is on the right of your table and as its sound starts resonating, listen carefully to any messages that you receive about what the 'eye' of your heart has seen.

Next, do the same thing with the singing bowl on the left of the table as you may gain further information about the journey. Then check that you are grounded by taking your awareness to your feet so you can consciously feel, beneath them, the floor of the room in your dwelling place in the material world.

Visualize roots going through Earth's Soul Chakra to Earth's Spirit Chakra so the knowledge that you have been given during the journey can be downloaded into them; for it is to be shared not only with your earthly companions, but also the World of Nature and Earth herself. The Divine loves all of Creation so deeply that when the Great Shift takes place, consciousness will be raised in human beings, birds, animals, and every sentient form that will be living on Earth.

Finally, affirm:-

I am protected and blessed
by the Loving Light of SHI
at all times.

Make sure that you are fully back in the material world by washing your hands and face in cold water and drinking a glass of water before you undertake any physical activities.

≡◇≡

Have faith and trust that all that is good will prevail. As soon as the Almighty One's Voice is heard, a great many blessings will be bestowed upon us. Our lives will be enriched in ways that we could not possibly imagine. Visions of the beauty of The Divine are without end and with each illumination the Peace of SHI, which passes all earthly understanding, is experienced.

The letter 'P' has been emphasized throughout the text. This is so that every time you see the letter 'P,' it reminds you of the word, 'PEACE.' Whenever you feel overwhelmed by the dramas occurring in the material world, the following meditation can help you to float above them.

Breathe in slowly to the count of two and feel your abdomen expanding as you breathe in.

◇

Hold your breath and with your inner voice say, 'Deep Peace within me.'

◇

Feel your abdomen contracting as you slowly breathe out to the count of three.

◇

Hold your breath and with your inner voice say,
'Deep Peace within all beings.'

◇

Slowly breathe in to the count of three.

◇

Hold your breath and with your inner voice say,
'Very Deep Peace within me.'

◇

Slowly breathe out to the count of four.

◇

Hold your breath and with your inner voice say,
'Very Deep Peace within all beings.'

◇

Slowly breathe in to the count of four.

◇

Hold your breath and with your inner voice say,
'Very, Very Deep Peace within me.'

◇

Slowly breathe out to the count of five.

◇

Hold your breath and with your inner voice say, 'Very, Very Deep Peace within all beings.'

◇

Know that you are protected and blessed by The Light at all times and gently close your eyes.

◇

See before you a magnificent fountain of crystal clear light that is surrounded by dancing sunbeams.

◇

Go and stand in the fountain and look up. Above the fountain there is a rainbow of the vivid colours of The Light. It is a sign of the New Covenant with Earth and its inhabitants. Notice how soothed you feel at seeing this Heavenly manifestation. As the fountain's light flows down and through you, all your cares just float away and your spirit starts dancing with joy.

◇

Take your awareness to your heart chakra now and sing the OM mantra with your inner voice as follows:-

ahhh-ahhh-ahhh-ahhh-ahhh-ahhh-ahhh
ooo-ooo-ooo-ooo-ooo-ooo-ooo
mmm-mmm-mmm-mmm-mmm-mmm-mmm

◇

A flame appears in your heart chakra that is like the flame in Jesus' heart chakra.

Study the flame very carefully.

◇

Look at the flame's golden glow

<>

Become aware that the warmth of the expression of the Great Soul's Love for you is pouring into your heart.

<>

Know, without a shadow of a doubt, that you are loved beyond measure endlessly, and that all will be well.

<>

Now, in the lovely rhythm of Oneness, chant the mantra, *'I am Divine Love'*

<>

When you are ready, slowly come back to your everyday awareness and once you open your eyes, make sure that you are thoroughly grounded before starting any activity.

Peace be with you

The benefits of meditating are well known. This meditation began in peace. Let it rest in your heart so that the feeling of peace lingers on and at the end of the day, may you still be feeling peaceful.

Portmanteau

$\mathcal{P}$assport

Along with breath exercises, mantras enable entry into the meditative state as well as helping spiritual growth; opening up spiritual insight, and facilitating advanced spiritual initiations. In other words, they are the passport for the journey that you have been on so that admittance could be gained to the Diamond Rung of the Ladder of Ascending Heart Consciousness. All the Sanskrit mantras in this book have been repeated numerous times, by numerous devotees of the transformative power of sound. They are pronounced as follows:-

PROLOGUE

The Jewel of Consciousness
is in the Heart Lotus

OM MANI PADME HUM
(om mah-nee-pahd-mey-hoom)

<>

PREPARATION

Salutations to the Great Purifier
Who purifies and protects
the sincere seeker

OM VAJRA SATTWA HUNG
(om vahj-rah saht-wah hoong)

◇

PATH

Salutations, Great Spiritual Teacher,
kindly steer us on to the path that
leads to the perfected being

OM NAMA SHIVAYA MANTRA
(om nah-mah shee-vah-yah)

◇

PILGRIMAGE

O Self-effulgent Light; Who has given birth
to all the spheres of consciousness, Who is
worthy of worship and appears through
the orbit of the Sun, illumine our intellect

GAYATRI MANTRA

OM BHUH, OM BHUVAHA, OM SWAHA,
OM MAHA, OM JANAHA, OM TAPAHA,
OM SATYAM, OM TAT SAVITUR VARENYAM
BHARGO DEVASYA DHIMAHI
DHIYO YONAHA PRACHODAYAT
(om boo om boo-vah-ha om swah-ha
om mah-ha om jah-nah-ha om tah-pah-ha
om saht-yahm om taht sah-vee-toor vahr-ehn-yum
bhahr-go deh-vahs-yah dee-mah-hee
dee-yoh yohn-ah-ha prah-choh-dah-yaht)

◇

PANORAMA

Salutations to the One,
for the power of the sound of the Voice of the One
brought Creation into being and the One is
the Bestower of all kinds of knowledge

OM EIM SARASWATIYEI SWAHA MANTRA
(om i'm sah-rah-swah-tee-yea swah-ha)

◇

PARTING

I Am Divine Love

AHAM PREMA MANTRA
(ah-hahm preh-mah)

◇

Most Eastern spiritual practices such as mantras are in the
Sanskrit Language. Each letter of the Sanskrit Language,
the Hebrew Language and the Holy Language of The
Light has a spiritual meaning. In The Cherishing
Language, the letter 'O' means, 'Absolute Love,' for 'O,'
or Source is the perfect circle in which everything is
contained.

Parlance

The Holy Language of The Light

One of the reasons why human beings have evolved in ways that other species on the physical plane have not is due to the languages that we speak. This is because the 'Word' brings everything into being. Apart from our national languages, special terminology is manifested to describe advances in fields such as technology, and so it is that in preparation for the ascension of the consciousness of the Human Race to the level of Divine Consciousness that was lost as a result of 'The Fall,' our re-attunement to The Holy Language of The Light will coincide with The Great Event. Indeed, The Event will be so great that it will result in a monumental journey into Divine Consciousness and in accordance with this, The Holy Language has been renamed, 'The Cherishing,' to herald the commencement of The Age of the Great Soul of Light Supreme. This will be when the wonder of Divine Love will be revealed to us in all its glory because we will be singing God's Song again.

The Language/Song was known to human beings at the beginning of our Civilization and since all of us were in direct contact with The Divine then it was not necessary to write down the Light-words, which have a higher vibration than the slower, denser vibrations of the words of our earthly languages. Over the centuries since 'The Fall,' though, the ability of the majority of us to hear The

Voice of The Almighty has diminished because the voice of the ego has taken precedence. The Light-words are being made known again to awaken those who are still asleep and in the dark, and to bring joy to those who are already awake and attuned to The Light. Illuminating and inspiring, the Light-words are currently encapsulating the forthcoming expansion of consciousness.

The development of human languages and our intense focus on material matters means that we do not have words that adequately describe matters of a spiritual nature; but the return of The Holy Language of The Light to the collective human consciousness will enable there to be greater cohesion because we will be able to speak with a unified voice of understanding about the Great Soul of Light Supreme and Divine Love. The seemingly paradoxical nature of the Higher World, which occurs when it is viewed from a dualistic level of perception, will be removed and our relationship with other Beings will be greatly enhanced.

Light-powers are intensified with heightened spiritual awareness, and telepathy will play a much larger part in our lives. This will mean our concept of language will change. The words of the languages of the physical world are often used to cause conflict; but the precious gift of soul expression is covered with many layers of light protection so that the Light-words cannot be used in this way.

The Light-words mean far more than it is possible to translate into our earthly languages at present; but remembrance of the meanings will gradually arise from deep within us because the knowledge is stored in the Light Body. Around the Language is an extra field that can only be detected by those who are able to appreciate the finer tuning of the vibrations. Once we are in harmony again with the dynamism of pure light thought, however, we will be able to go deeper and deeper into the meanings of the sounds and more levels of The Holy Language will start to be opened up to us. Our realization of the World of Spirit will, by then, have progressed to the level where the significance of the divine meanings of the Light-words will be understood leading to a wealth of knowledge being gained about The Light.

After being in abeyance for so long, the Light-words will come in a slow trickle; but as understanding of them grows the transmissions will increase until a steady stream of them is obtained. As the framework of The Holy Language takes form in our minds, and our re-awakening to it progresses, The Cherishing Language will be revealed in its true form; for a fast flowing river of visions of the World of Light accompany the higher vibrations as they are expressed. Although the power of the vibrations will be unleashed and cosmic consciousness will be opened up, we will not be able to engage in a higher level of communion with The Almighty until our hearts are filled with compassion, tenderness, understanding, peace and love for all of Creation.

The Light-words are conveyed slowly, softly, and with grace and dignity. They flow from the Heart Chakra in the rhythm of the beautiful cadence of the Sacred Heart. Many of the sounds are elongated and are expressed as though they are being emitted from a deep sigh of bliss. Some are held at a certain pitch; others rise in the same way that a musical scale does, all of them are expressed lovingly. Although our voices will not have the range that would enable us to sing them out loud in the beautiful way the Angels sing them, we will be able to sing the higher harmonies with our inner voices.

The Language is called The Cherishing because it is the expression of the outpouring of the warmth of the Love of SHI. God's Love is expressed in every letter of every word thereby increasing the love that is in our hearts. There is nothing to fear by singing the words of God's Love Song as love will come from our hearts as every Light-word is sounded. The vibration of love will then resonate and keep resonating as we call to other souls. In turn, this will have an effect on the whole of the Human Race. The Light-words will reverberate in our Heart Chakras at the frequency that will cause our connection to The Light to be enhanced as well. The Language will, therefore, play a vital role in elevating the collective consciousness of humanity.

Although it will require deep reflection on the meanings of the Light-words before our human selves are fully attuned to the higher harmonies of Spirit, a big change of lifestyle will result from the re-building of our awareness of The Cherishing Language. When we listen to the Light-words with our hearts, the Light-words will be able to shine through with their blessings. Differences in cultures will meld; ignorance in the form of racism will disappear; opinion will be re-formed; any dissonance will be rapidly forgotten; disparity will cease, and gender bias will be straightened out.

In order for there to be harmony in the physical world, the male and female energies need to be equally balanced. The use of the following Light-words will help to cement the change in our perception of gender.

ATESH (ahhh-teshhh (rhymes with mesh)) – Great Master

EESH (ee-eshhh (rhymes with (r/w) mesh)) – Angel

ERESH (er-eshhh (r/w mesh)) - An Individual's Spirit

EYESH (ee-yesh (r/w mesh)) - Archangel

MERESH (mur-esh (r/w mesh)) - Human Being

MERRESH (mur-resh (r/w mesh)) - Ascended Master

MESHET (me^ (as in met)-sheet) - An Individual's Soul

YISH (eye-ee-shhh) – SHI, EORRESH YAVOY, Source

The Light-words are often expressed as mantras. For example, the mantra AT NOM (art – nom (r/w from) means, 'Spirit, manifest in my being greater understanding of The Light.'

$\mathcal{P}$rofile

Listen to the echo in your heart,
move within its re-echoing.
Let your breath become the extension
of the echo and your voice the sound of Heaven.
Let all rise as a mantra of purest kind.

REV. ROSEMARY ADDISON

I was taught how to meditate at the Maharishi Mahesh Yogi School of Transcendental Meditation in Kent. The Transcendental Method involves repeating spiritualized sounds, or mantras, from the ancient Sanskrit language of India to calm the mind so a deeper level of meditation can be accessed. After very many repetitions of the mantras, enlightenment is eventually gained. All the information in CRYSTAL MYSTICISM was obtained purely through meditation techniques. I have never used hallucinogenic drugs of any kind.

There is a saying that when the student is ready, the teacher appears. Several years after I had moved from Kent to Sussex, I met Rev. Rosemary Addison. She was an Interfaith Minister and she shared with me a method of meditation that she had developed. It consisted of using three meditational aids at the same time – gazing at a lovely photograph of a flower, whilst listening to the special sonic effects on the tracks of the compact disc that she gave me and repeating, as a mantra, the word, 'God,' with my inner voice.

Approximately six months after I started using Rosemary's meditation method, Light-words from The Holy Language of The Light, which is usually referred to as, The Cherishing Language, started being conveyed to me along with information about the Great Event. I was totally overwhelmed by this experience, let alone the nature of the knowledge that I was being given, but Rosemary was very supportive. She particularly liked the positive news that was coming through about the New Dawn of The Light of the World.

So much love accompanies communications from The Divine and I spent many happy hours, when Rosemary visited me, listening to the streams of pure consciousness that she had received during her meditations. It was as though I was at my true home on those occasions. I was completely in tune with what Rosemary was sharing with me.

After a long and very courageous battle with cancer, Rosemary suddenly became very ill. She passed over to the World of Spirit after I had known her for six years. One morning, about a week later, I was about to begin the prayers that I say after I have meditated when Rosemary appeared. She looked even more radiant than when she was in her physical body, which was the first thing that people always noticed about Rosemary. The second thing was her wonderful presence. It made you feel as though you were enveloped in the special relationship that she had with God.

I gained great comfort from looking at Rosemary's beaming face again. She looked so well, which erased the sadness that was in me from seeing the suffering that she had had to endure. In the months that followed, I saw Rosemary several times in her physical form, whilst I was dreaming. Since then, I have seen her on a number of occasions in her risen form when I have been meditating. Every year, I light a candle on Rosemary's birthday, which was 23rd December, rather than marking the date of her transition, and give thanks for being blessed with meeting a teacher who brought a profound change to my life in such a special way. The Light-words of The Cherishing Language still flow to me during my morning meditations and every so often, I receive further information about the Great Event from various Light Bearers.

Rosemary   Lindsey

$\mathcal{P}$ublications

Eason, Cassandra
THE NEW CRYSTAL BIBLE
Carlton Books Ltd., 2010

Govert, Johndennis and Hara, Hapi
THE CINTAMANI CRYSTAL MATRIX:
QUANTUM INTENTION AND THE
WISH-FULFILLING GEM
Destiny Books, 2022

Hall, Judy
CRYSTAL SKULLS
Red Wheel/Weiser, LLC, 2016

Raven, Hazel
SACRED CRYSTALS
Quatro Publishing plc, 2017

Raven, Hazel
CRYSTAL HEALING: A VIBRATIONAL JOURNEY
THROUGH THE CHAKRAS
Raven & Co. Publishing, 2000

Simmons, Robert,
THE ALCHEMY OF STONES
Destiny Books, 2020

Simmons, Robert and Warner, Kathy
MOLDAVITE: STARBORN STONE OF
TRANSFORMATION
Heaven and Earth Books, 1988

Ashley-Farrand, Thomas
HEALING MANTRAS
Gateway, 2000

Day, Lindsey Elizabeth and
Lawrence, Marion (Spiritual Artist)
ATLANTIS: AS BELOW SO ABOVE*
A SPIRITUAL ODYSSEY
The Cloister House Press, 2021

Gray, Kyle
DIVINE MASTERS, ANCIENT WISDOM
Hay House, 2021

Yogananda, Paramahansa
AUTOBIOGRAPHY OF A YOGI
Self-Realization Fellowship, 1999

Yogananda, Paramahansa
THE YOGA OF JESUS
Self-Realization Fellowship, 2019

*There is more information in this book about the Great Event

*P*rovidence

One morning, whilst I was meditating, Melchizedek appeared. He was holding up his crystal lamp and he gave me a crystal that I had never seen before. After I had been attuned to the stone, I learned about its properties, but I was not made aware of the crystal's name.

After the meditation had finished, I picked up my copy of Cassandra Eason's book, 'The New Crystal Bible.' Mystically, the book fell open at the page where there was a photograph that was exactly like the crystal that I had just seen. It was called, '*Titanite*.'

For everything there is a time and almost six months passed by before I was able to buy the stone. This was because my attempts to obtain the crystal kept being thwarted. It was not long after Brexit and an order that I had placed for the *Titanite* on Amazon was turned back at customs due to various petty problems. When I looked for stockists on the Internet, I only found one that sold *Titanite* and it turned out that the stone was no longer in stock.

One day, though, I became aware that purchasing a copy of the 'Soul & Spirit' Magazine would be helpful. In it there were many adverts for crystal websites, but my attention was drawn to the following one:-

KSC CRYSTALS
PO Box 415,
Wilmslow,
Cheshire,
SK9 0EQ
01625 250345

www.ksccrystals.com
keithbirch@totalise.co.uk

When I accessed the website of KSC Crystals, I was very pleased to discover that there was a selection of *Titanite* stones. I found one that looked like the one I had been shown and it arrived the next day expertly packaged by Keith Birch's wife, Sandra.

Keith sends out a weekly newsletter that contains photographs and details about certain crystals that are available on the website and he is happy to take orders over the telephone. It is an uplifting experience to speak to Keith. He is a man of wise words, good advice and integrity and his love for, and understanding of, crystals shines through when you talk to him. Although it is not always part of the service that other stockists provide, Keith is always willing to share his knowledge about crystals. He will give you guidance on the crystals that work well together; the best way to access the properties of some of the stones and provide you with all kinds of helpful information, if you ask him.

Crystals have opened up many things for me in unexpected ways. They have all turned out to be providential.

$\mathcal{P}$rediction

As a result of Earth's Great Shift, *Tantermani*, the *Fiery Stones* that were the foundations of the greatness of the Atlantean Civilisation at its peak, will be found. They will be discovered in tunnels and caves alongside minerals that have been kept safe in them for thousands of years.

Tantermani have an intricate construction. Their shape is similar to crystals that have been fashioned to represent the Merkabah/Merkavah, which means, Chariot of God; but they have more 'angles' on the outside. The stones are white and they glisten as though the sun is shining on an icy surface; but in the centre of the numerous intersections that are inside the stones there is a flame. Its fiery appearance denotes the intensity of the mystical powers that these heavenly extraterrestrial stones possess and they have to be handled with great care.

The *Tantermani* Light Bearers will assist in the building of a renewed, more profound, existence on Earth. In some ways it will mirror the level that was possessed by Atlanteans, who had the powers to bring about miraculous occurrences with the help of the *Tantermani*. The powers that will be regained will not, however, be able to be misused as they will be re-programmed, in connection with Humanity's Great Shift, so that they can only be used for the good of all.

This Great Event will be happening soon. Sleep peacefully until it occurs. Then rise with joy, for all will be well.

$\mathcal{P}$rayer

≡◇≡

May the Angel of Hope
always be by your side
and may all your
journeys be
blessed.

≡◇≡

CPSIA information can be obtained
at www.ICGtesting.com
Printed in the USA
BVHW061016231222
654916BV00023B/994